The Relief of Unknowing

Unconditional Love Appears as

Potent Vibrant Aliveness

Also by Jim Galbraith

The Freedom of Unknowing

No-Thing

Every-Thing

Just Living the Freedom of Unknowing

The Relief of Unknowing

Unconditional Love Appears as
Potent Vibrant Aliveness

Jim Galbraith

© 2019 by Jim Galbraith

All rights reserved

ISBN--13: 978-0-578-46719-1

ISBN--10: 0-578-46719-4

Potent Aliveness is 'This' Already

Contents

Contents

Preface

Relief might imply a satisfying full breath in and out; however, in this context solace connotes unimpaired freedom!

The ease of 'This', the mystery of unconditional love, is indescribable. The ineffable, inconceivable, utterly obvious joy and pain of sparkling vitality is 'This' which is already untamed, radiant energy.

Wildness shops for food, pays the bills, exercises at the athletic club, works around the house; enjoyment or agitation might arise but the emergence of either one is apparent and happens for no one.

The comfort or aggravation, of nothing being better or worse than anything else, is potent freedom that cannot be crafted into words.

That does not mean 'I' go around with twinkling eyes and an obnoxious *knowing* grin on 'my' face.

No.

Everything looks and appears the same.

'This' freedom of unknowing is just that.

It is unknowable.

The relief is not an experience and not a body sensation or mental construct of some sort.

It is not something in the foreground or background.

In 'my' second book an attempt was made to communicate, as this unknowing freedom, with 'you' the reader.

However, there is no 'I' here to communicate with a 'you' there.

The suggestion or idea that there is no one, never has been nor will there ever be anyone, does not make sense to most people.

Therefore, 'I' rarely share the message found within these pages.

This book may challenge belief systems held true for generations. Don't worry, there is nothing being disputed nor is there anything being taught.

What is being suggested could seem scary or a bit fearful to that *thing* which believes it is real.

…however, that *thing* is illusory!

That *thing* calls itself 'me' or 'I'; hence, apostrophes around the pronouns '*I*', '*you*', '*me*' or the noun '*Jim*' etc. connote this illusion throughout the book.

'I' or 'me', however, does not believe it is illusory; it experiences itself as real!

'I' or 'me' seems to have practical contact with and observation of facts and events in a world perceived as authentic.

It believes it was born and that it will die.

The tension felt and held in the body seems to prove its existence.

'I' or 'me' can't get that it is only wholeness '*I*' *ing,* only the absolute '*me*' *ing.*

It can't get that it is not separate from the absolute.

It can't fathom the idea of non-dualism.

So, the 'I' or 'me' searches, explores, pursues, hunts, seeks, probes, investigates, inquires, examines, scrutinizes, digs etc.

It finds something...for a while.

...but it doesn't know that what it is actually seeking is the end of itself!

Round and round it goes.

 Touching actually...

...an invitation to derision.

...for there is no 'me' to have an end to itself--ever!

...merely an illusion seeking solidity.

Nothing pretending to be something for a little while.

Disorder created by the 'I' is seen worldwide.

The hollowness...

Scarecrows packed with tawny straw...

Snow men and women with carrot noses and button eyes...

...that walk and talk

...pretending, impersonating, bluffing

...improvising, acting, faking

...who melt into each other's arms

...crying

"Who am I?"

"What's it all about?"

"What's going on?"

"Why can't I get this?"

"Please show me the way!"

Fear not, you are still safe. This book will show and give you no advice or answers.

...and guess what?

There is no 'you' to learn anything.

Congratulations.

You have found a book that might as well be all blank pages.

Make it your *pet book.*

Your little secret.

'I' won't tell...

Thank you for purchasing this precious gem which is priceless and worthless simultaneously. May it comfort, scare, entice or simply make you laugh.

Perhaps the relief of unknowing will arise while 'you' gaze at the cover or god forbid, read a page!

The Relief of Unknowing

Unconditional Love Appears as
Potent Vibrant Aliveness

Introduction

Do you like scary rides?

Are you a thrill seeker?

Maybe you are looking for something to eliminate continual thoughts of "The good old days" that seem to be driving you into a chaotic, uncertain future.

Perhaps you are wonderfully normal and simply just want a little peace of mind.

Possibly the persistent feeling of faking it seems to dance in your background; the search to find *the real you* in people, places and things continues.

Perchance there is no *real* you!

Conceivably 'you' and 'I' are illusory and 'we' make absolutely no difference in an imagined world. The likelihood that 'we' and a real world are hollow creations of the brain may be the source of our sleepless nights.

What can we do to obviate this terrifying possibility?

Can we give up, turn over or surrender this life to a higher power, religion, guru, mahatma or enlightened teacher?

If the 'self is, indeed, illusory--who would give up or surrender?

Who would chant, fast, donate to charity or become austere to attain liberation?

Many have tried!

Is science of any help?

With billions, trillions of dollars, scientists have found nothing to support the reality of 'self'.

Some neuroscientists, as a matter of fact, are finding more evidence that points to the illusion of self.

Many of us know, down deep, that 'our' ego, the fallacious 'I' or 'me', usually wants just one thing.

...one thing!

'I', 'me' or 'self' yearns to be free.

Which...

...is impossible!

What is being suggested in this writing is this:

There is no self to become free.

But the self doesn't know that.

How could it?

It does not exist.

There is no 'self'.

There is a felt tension in an apparent body that seems to experience internal and external stimuli. In turn, the brain converts this tensity into an 'I', 'me' or 'self' in which it takes its stand in an apparent world.

...but, its stance does not produce abiding satisfaction.

Inevitably, the 'me' seeks to fill the seeming, unsatisfactory void with that which it thinks will gratify its hunger.

So, dear seeker…

Peel off another layer.

Believe in an afterlife.

Trust in life after life.

Rely on 'your' own intimate experience.

Become enlightened.

Live in the divine bliss of the holy name.

Be *knowingly* the light of pure awareness.

…and when all that ends, keep at it, you've come this far.

Believe until the sun supernovas.

You want to hang onto that ego?

Be my guest.

No one will stop you.

It's the thing to do.

Jesus will save you.

Ramana Maharshi's videos will inspire you…

However, in this apparent sharing there will be no tolerance for *so-called* teachers complicit in upholding the belief that the self, relying on its own intimate experience, can somehow collapse and emerge into liberation or enlightenment.

This message points to the utterly obvious:

There is no self to collapse and, of course, no self to become liberated or enlightened.

Potent, vibrant aliveness seems to arise from that which is whole and complete.

There is just this ineffable freedom ringing, singing, dancing...

...just this which is absolute, wild and free, apparently appearing as anything and everything.

...unconditional love arising in a myriad of shapes and forms.

...wholeness sans separation.

...just 'This', 'simply 'This'.

...there is just what is apparently happening for no one.

No life.

No death.

Just this indescribable aliveness.

Passionately free.

No creation or destruction.

Just 'This' which can appear as chaos or tranquility but cannot be defined as either.

...and so, there is nothing the apparent person will fear. Whatever arises, in any and all apparent situations, is open and free. It is **all** special.

There is nothing to attain, because 'This' is it already.

There is nothing to seek and, obviously, nothing to find.

Unconditional love, wholeness, certainty, the absolute, is 'This' which is timeless and space less.

No past, present or future.

There is just what is happening for no one.

Reading these pages happens but no one reads.

Don't expect any answers; however, many questions may arise.

Everything is perfect *just as it is*!

If questions do arise, that is also *just as it is*!

It is all so vigorously alive and free.

What a relief!

For no one.

Relief of Unknowing

Relief from the disquiet of knowing seems to be the number one factor in attempting to share this message.

It's not that 'I' or 'we' stick our heads in the sand and pretend that everything *just goes away*.

It is obvious there is no 'I' or 'we' to cover one's apparent eyes and ears, chant a magic mantra and wake up in bed, free of the anxiety and stress of the seeming world.

Unknowing would seem to be the *key*.

...but it isn't.

There is no finding nor can the apparent individual seek 'This' which is always already.

'I' was once asked by Mahatma Rageshwaranand, "Have you ever taken psychedelics?"

It seemed a rude and strange question.

After a significant pause he began to chuckle.

"Temporary relief, temporary relief for the West," as he continued chuckling.

Looking around today at the opioid epidemic, it appears that scores of people are openly seeking *temporary relief.*

It seems most folks seek and receive a short-term reprieve from the myriad forms of angst available anywhere-anytime.

Short term is short term.

One cycle after another.

One lot after another.

One pill or substance after another.

One (fill in the blank) -------------------- after another.

The relief, spoken in this discourse, is not even relief.

It is better!

Relief appears to require a somebody that experiences a feeling of reassurance and relaxation.

When that somebody is no more and recognizes (without recognizing) that 'he' or 'she' was never a 'he' or 'she' in the first place; relief is spelled *unknowing*.

'I' just cannot help but laugh.

It is so obvious and simple.

The relief.

Oh, the relief.

The wonderful, soothing, liberating relief of unknowing releases 'me' from 'myself'.

However, saying it like that makes it sound like an apparent person can get *unknowing*.

Sorry, but getting what cannot be known is impossible.

It's funny, 'I' am not trying to convince anybody.

'I' am just (pause) relieved of all burden.

That does not mean apparent hardships and difficulties cease to arise. They do, every day.

It's just that, well...

An apparent eagle, or maybe it was a heron, just flapped by skimming the tree tops.

'I' cannot give 'you' direction or guidance in discovering the seeming comfort and well being of the freedom in which these apparent words imply.

Wholeness is not separated into parts. There is no 'I' over here writing or speaking to a 'you' over there.

It could be said 'Jim' was relieved, but that's not quite right. How could 'he' have been comforted; 'he' never was in the first place.

Clearly, no one can direct someone to the relief of unknowing. There is just unknowing.

...and there is not something that is unknown that knows that.

Language is so...limited.

It's the relaxation.

Deep breath in...

...the relaxation.

...freedom from tension and anxiety.

...deep breath out.

The rest, the deep satisfying feeling of being well rested.

Not tired.

Alert.

Focused.

Attentive.

For no reason.

For nobody.

No 'I' to be alert, attentive or focused; yet all three arise for no one.

A magical mystery, unknowable and unattainable, seems to appear as vivid aliveness for no one.

The relief screams it out, laughs it up, writes its name on your forehead.

'This' is it honey-child!

Writing for Nothing

…or maybe, writing arises from nothing.

There certainly is no one here who is trying to make a point or communicate in some way.

That which is 'This' already cannot be transferred. How could it and where would it go?

Writing is apparently happening, but that's it, nothing else. There is no 'me' sitting here trying to explain to 'you' what 'This' is.

The pleasure of writing is 'This'.

The apparent 'I', composing these seeming words and phrases, simply enjoys writing; even better, enjoyment arises for no one.

It does not matter if these words are ever read by anyone. It is obvious there actually is no *anyone* in the first place!

Nothing appearing as writing.

Nothing arising as reading.

Nothing to be learned or gained from anything said or not said in this message.

No one sitting here trying to tell you how it is, or what you should or should not do.

No teaching.

Thank God!

No pedanticism.

Thinking happens and seems to stop the process of writing.

Writing happens and appears to stop the process of thinking.

No beginning.

No ending

No middle either.

The lovely apparent process of aliveness writing for nothing.

Nothing to get.

'This' is already *it*.

Essentially, this is the mystery, shouting at you, "Hello"!

Hello!

That's not quite right either, for what could even shout at you?

Well, the mystery can appear any way it wants. It is free and wild.

Wild!

If it's free and wild and says, "Hello".

Wow!

It shouts as the sun, moon and rain.

It roars as the air 'we' breathe and howls as all of 'our' aches and pains.

Nothing and everything (known or unknown) whispers, "This' is it already!"

Why, why would anyone search for what already is?

Ludicrous, to say the least!

Ego Exposed

Obviously:

The ego, also known as 'I', 'me' or 'self' is illusory. It is not what it seems to be.

One theory suggests that from a very early age, before we can even walk, the human being begins to create an 'I', a <u>made-up</u> existence, that lasts him or her a lifetime!

A child can be taught anything and will believe those teachings. What is made up is believed to be real.

Video games have a reality factor that can keep a toddler or grown kid occupied and deeply involved day in and day out. The game is played, yet the involvement, that which is at stake (usually life or death) is total.

What is apparently happening in the world is no different than a sophisticated video game. Seeming people believing themselves to be real, playing the game of "Live or Die in my Neighborhood".

A human being remains a child, vulnerable and susceptible to parents, peers, spouses, teachers, siblings, culture, religion, environment, politics, employers etc. until apparent death takes his or her body. The game is played, yet never won or lost.

There is no point in asking why it all seems to happen. No satisfactory answer will ever arise.

Seeking an answer will simply usurp one's life.

There are some who know the ego is not real. They really get it. Like everything else, they want to <u>own</u> it, tell others of their great illumination.

Nonsense!

Who is there to know?

What is there to get?

How could one own that which is not here or there?

Exposing the ego is essentially some sort of hocus-pocus. What is there to expose and to whom would it be revealed?

The communication suggested in this message is impossible to grasp.

However, speakers making money on their tours of the world, internet broadcasts and books claiming non-duality is real or unreal are popping up everywhere.

Feed something to the apparent seeker, that makes no sense and promises nothing, fills the pockets of those that are "getting in" while the "getting's good."

One female internet speaker demands that you *pay* for her *free* broadcasts.

"Pay down here," she says, while posing provocatively and blowing smoke at the camera.

Another picks his nose and, of course, says nothing.

No one will read what is apparently being written with these apparent words. Seeming fingers dash across a keyboard, but nothing of any value bubbles forth with knowledge that can help one find his or her way.

There is no <u>him</u> or <u>her</u> to find a way.

How do 'I' know this.

'I' have said it over and over and over…

There is no 'I' who knows anything of what is being written in these words and <u>so-called</u> statements.

Apparent words are written.

That's it.

The apparent 'I' can call its seeming self a character, but that is just another way of identifying as something.

There is no something that is something.

There is simply 'This'…

Indescribable freedom.

Even saying it as indescribable freedom makes it sound like 'I' have this freedom.

'I' do not have this freedom.

There is no 'I' to be free.

You see?

There is just no point in trying to comprehend the content of this message.

There is no freedom, yet the only word that seems to work in this discourse is freedom.

Thank God for this freedom.

My God!

Thank you for this freedom.

'I don't mean a singular God out there somewhere. It's just the way the thank you is arising.

Thank you unconditional love for this freedom.

Thank you wholeness for this freedom.

Thank you, thank you, thank you!

The wonder and awe of essentially nothing being everything sings the song of uncompromising love to and for no one.

God, 'I' never dreamed happiness could be this way.

So rich, so full, so complete and yet, for no one!

No 'I', no 'self', simply wholeness appearing as the lovely rain, whispering wind and a silver haired Capricorn wading through nettles and cold water.

Laughing sometimes.

Crying sometimes.

One breath in.

One breath out.

Apparently.

There is Nothing to Say

Sitting, gazing, thoughts arising, silence—simply this on a typical Saturday afternoon.

One could imply, "This is magic—a magic moment."

...but, there is no moment and the freedom, the relief of unknowing sings as the woodpecker in the distance and the sun reflecting from leaves wet with recent rainfall.

'This' timeless, open aliveness is all there is and, of course, all there is not.

No one is saying this and there is no truth being revealed.

There is wonderfully 'This', as electric green foliage, from a seeming tree called the Large Leaf Maple, mirrors golden sunlight.

A satisfying breath and the apparent body content and at ease.

No story can form from 'This', which is always already.

'This' is what is happening.

Nothing is happening—everything is happening.

There are no events to be known, watched or observed, for there is no separate 'me' standing apart that could do so.

The floor creaks above 'me'. An apparent neighbor hitting all the squeaky spots he seemingly can. His washing machine begins its noisy cycle.

'This' is what is happening.

Nothing is happening—everything is happening.

Rising.

Rising.

Rising.

The freedom of unknowing appears as some-thing and no-thing simultaneously.

Atomic-number-54.

Noble gas.

Helium.

Unnecessary in an ascension to paradise for no one.

Unknowingly Seeking

How can the apparent individual unknowingly seek something? It would seem one would have to know what he or she was seeking before the searching process could begin.

That is not the case.

We begin as babies fresh and complete—whole. There is just what is happening, sans personality or illusory ego.

Along the way something happens that seems to result in an illusory separation from the absolute.

Wholeness seems to break into pieces.

It appears that something relative arises and reveals itself as 'me' or 'I' and 'others'.

The self-enquiry teacher will advise going back, way back to when this separation occurred; become one with that seeming separation.

In so doing the illusory self can drop away and wholeness, completeness will result.

Again, the assumption that the 'I' or 'me' is real drives this theory. How can something that does not exist in the first place break apart?

Then, go back?

Back to where?

Space and time play into this idealistic formula, when, in actuality, going back or forward is conjecture.

The seeker believes that an actual separation occurs. What could separate and from what?

Nothing happened, nothing happens, and nothing will happen; however, this sentence implies time and is, therefore, not quite right either.

There is simply 'This'.

The absolute appearing as the relative.

...and there are no parts or pieces.

The illusory 'I' just imagines itself and the world to be fragmented which sparks its initial search for wholeness before it can even talk!

Unknowing seeking begins...

A Large Brain

There is no 'I'.

There is no 'you'.

There is no 'world'.

No explanation needed.

Utterly obvious.

To or for whom?

No to, for or whom.

Just this inexplicable aliveness.

Thoughts arising.

Apparent actions happening.

Sameness apparently repeating it-self often?

There is simply seeming, wonderful sameness that does not begin or end.

This incredible sameness can be called wholeness.

This inexplicable wholeness might be called one, but that does not work; one implies separation into possible parts.

That which is non-dual can be called nothing.

That which is nothing disappears as a word and has no value even in thought.

Therefore, it could not repeat itself?

How could that which is not two repeat itself?

Repeating an everyday activity does appear real.

The human brain is huge, bigger than any other species on this apparent planet.

This enormous organ, of soft nervous tissue contained in the skull, functions as the coordinating center of sensation, intellect and nervous activity.

It is so sophisticated that the 'me' or 'I' **it creates** experiences itself to be real.

Of course it feels real; there is a 'me' or 'I' seemingly present to verify its existence.

It knows it is real.

Down deep, it doesn't know it is real.

...<u>that</u> is its problem.

It pretends to know, but all along it doesn't know.

The brain assimilates what it believes is of apparent value, supports this judgment of what it *thinks* is most important; then it looks forward to continual survival.

The 'me' or 'I' is created by the brain. 'It' feels. It experiences. It doesn't believe it is real. The tension of the five senses and the reinforcement of thought give it the power of apparent awareness or consciousness, which appears as its own intimate, direct experience.

Nevertheless, it still searches and explores for that *something* that is missing.

It builds its identity over an apparent lifetime and will defend itself to its death to reinforce the reality of its selfhood, often ignoring the pain that smolders in the solar plexus.

It is so obvious!

A huge brain creates a huge ego.

A huge ego believes it has a real identity with free will and choice.

The brain creates.

The ego experiences.

The apparent world suffers.

What's really crazy is the belief that the self, our identity, is going to die.

How can something that is made up of memories, sensations and anticipations die?

Does a make-believe creature actually die?

How could it?

Same thing with the so-called ego.

It simply cannot die because it has never been alive in the first place.

The large brain of the human keeps creating; look at the condition of the apparent world.

Shouldn't that be proof enough?

No.

As long as the illusory 'self' experiences itself as real, it and the apparent world will continue its downward spiral.

Over and Over

There is nothing being said in this discourse and the same message is being expressed in seeming different ways throughout this apparent book.

How could anything be said?

There is no one here to say anything and certainly no one there to hear or read these seeming words.

It seems like there is someone here and there but there is not.

Sophisticated video games should be enough proof of that fact.

'I' was driving my grandson (who plays video games day and night) to an appointment. It was clear that driving him to the desired destination was no different for him than riding his video horse to the hide-out shack in the forest.

There was no real horse, just as there was no real car heading for an appointment.

The brain creates the illusion of 'me' and it does not matter what seems to show up. The body will serve the brain and the brain will serve the body in maintaining the tension needed in feeling and experiencing the 'self' as real.

It is somewhat easier to see the illusive nature inherent in a video game; not so easy in maneuvering a heavy vehicle through crowded streets and highways.

Actually, there is no game being played, for no players exist.

Who or what plays the apparent game?

One could say wholeness constricts into an apparent player and the seeming tension that appears in the body feels real.

This apparent real feeling translates into 'I' feel; therefore, 'I' am playing the game.

Nothing, however, is happening. Cars roll, wind howls, rain falls, flags fly; yet, no game can or will ever be played.

Most humans believe the tension held in the body, the felt constriction, translates into a 'me' living and functioning in a 'real' world, playing a real game.

Play jobs, families, religions and governments stand firm and support this illusion with uncompromising loyalty.

Anywhere and everywhere seeming people play electronic devices as if they were reality itself.

Heads down, bent--contorted necks, arthritic fingers...

Play.

Play.

Play!

Who wins?

Who loses?

Who gains?

No one.

No one ever plays.

Who knows this to be true?

No one.

There is no truth to be known for there is no one to know that truth.

Is what is being suggested in this writing real?

How could it be when nothing real exists?

Why write or speak in this manner?

No why or reason exists for anything to be written.

Is reading this a waste of time?

No, for time does not exist (except for getting to an appointment on time or for a football game).

Just joking...

All there is--**is** 'This'.

The apparent games being played are only 'This' which is and is not.

What is being sought, through all the fun, is love itself just as it is and, of course, just as it is not.

Out of a Job

Fired!

That's not quite true.

How could something, that never had a job in the first place, be given its *marching orders?*

The *full-time job* of maintaining the 'me' seems very real indeed.

…until there is no longer a 'me'!

Who employs this 'me'?

Why does it seemingly run rampant on this apparent planet?

Those in poverty say, "Why 'me'?"

Those that have billions say, "Look at 'me'!"

Those in the middle say, "Woe is 'me'."

This 'mc' is apparently self-employed.

The bigger and more confident it is, the more money and status it seems to enjoy.

The smaller and seemingly less self-assured it is, limited money and poor ranking it appears to dislike.

The 'me' has never held a job in the first place; yet, it unwaveringly believes it is working hard.

It believes it is working so hard...so hard!

For *crying out loud*!

The 'me' is not real.

It is a ------- (insert your favorite expletive) illusion!

Illusions are not what they appear to be.

The 'me' is not what it appears to be.

'I' don't care if it claims to be the richest man or woman in modern history; the 'me' is not what it appears to be.

So what if it makes two dollars a day or two billion dollars a day?

So what if it is homeless or lives in a hundred-million-dollar mansion?

It is not real to live in either of those places; but it believes it to be so.

Good god! Look at the condition of the apparent world.

Shouldn't that be proof enough of the absolute absurdity of the 'me' believing itself to be real?

A pretend person, living in a pretend world, doing a pretend job.

The only thing 'I' am going to say is this:

The 'me' is illusory; it is a psychosomatic misunderstanding.

Simple.

It does not help to know this, but when the 'me' is no longer, when it is *out of a job*, as it were, it is blatantly obvious there is only the absolute.

That which is relative appears to arise in the absolute; this constricted tension in the body appears as 'me', 'I', 'self' etc.

The 'me' thinks it is gainfully employed and doing a *bang-up* job!

All along there is only the absolute, wholeness, pure aliveness--that which is simply happening.

There never was, is or will be a 'me'.

Maybe 'you' can somehow get over yourself...

...perhaps *Fire* that deadbeat 'me'.

Maybe you can look at your apparent self in the mirror and laugh!

Laugh like you have never laughed before.

Laugh so hard you don't know who or where you even are.

..and when you are through, laugh some more at the freedom you now enjoy without the dictator (also known as 'me') calling the shots!

Do it now.

'I' mean it!

Do it right now!

Darn, if it was only that simple 'I' could make a fortune *freeing* people

Alas, it won't matter.

There is no 'you' to become free.

But watch it, even when there is no apparent 'me' emotions still arise.

If anger arises, that's what's happening.

Since there is no 'you' to embrace anger, desire or attachment, there is no 'you' to give any of those three to god or guru or therapist.

There is unambiguous anger, desire, or attachment apparently happening without a beginning, middle or end.

An emotion is and isn't, so there is no comment like, "Oh, just *ride it out,* or it *will pass,* or *I can live with this forever."*

The 'me' is plainly *out of a job* that it (which never was) never had.

Why does Wholeness...

...suffer

...discriminate

...kill aimlessly

...go to war

...lie

...cheat

...steal

...create monstrosities

...take sides

...make up religions

...get addicted to drugs?

The list could go on and on...

There is no answer to these questions.

Wholeness is wild and free. It has form, yet it is formless.

It is not a something that plans or pictures or creates.

It (and it's not an it) seems to appear as any one of the aforementioned, but because it is free there is no limit or restriction as to what may or may not appear to manifest to or for the apparent human form.

Why is wholeness writing these words?

There is no way to answer or address such questions.

There is no direction given, so the human brain makes up a direction.

Suffering appears to happen; the human brain and body *pop* a painkiller for relief.

People want to be saved.

The human brain accommodates itself with designer religions.

Fear drives the multitudes!

Lying, cheating, stealing, killing apparently provide a temporary "Out" to perceived real or unreal circumstances.

There are no answers, just as there are no questions.

There is just what is and is not for an apparent someone.

However, there is no one...

The apparent reader will verify, however, that there is someone reading this.

When it is said there is no one, it is not meant to be insulting, rather wholeness seeming to speak from the quiet of nothing and everything.

So much apparent noise.

My god, the noise!

Where is the quiet?

That's just the thing.

It's quiet, so quiet...still...peaceful; yet, apparent noise anywhere and everywhere.

No one knows it is quiet and still, just as no one knows it is chaotic and coming apart.

There is no one here who knows what is being suggested.

Wholeness appearing to write these words for no one.

Why?

It's just what is apparently happening.

Isn't that just the brain making all this up?

That could be said, yes.

Just another dreamed up idea in someone's head?

That could also be said, yes.

Then, what is the point?

No point.

Why bother reading or discussing this?

Exactly!

Ludicrous.

...but, you are writing a book.

No, sorry, but a book is being written...apparently.

So many ideas and opinions!

Seems so, doesn't it?

Yes, it certainly does.

Sit back in your loneliness and just cry.

You think that will help?

Sure.

OK then.

Feeling better?

I couldn't cry.

That happens (apparently).

I'm laughing a bit though,

Laughter is good.

This has got to be the strangest book anyone will ever read!

I know!

No one will read it though.

Isn't that great!

No worries!

No one writing and no one reading.

What could be better than that?

Nothing to gain and nothing to lose?

Right!

Who would gain and who would lose?

Jeez. I'm feeling a lot better.

Yay!

Family and Friends

People seem to think that if there is no longer a 'me' or an 'I', a great disservice will befall one's family and certainly interfere with friends and relationships.

This, of course, is what the 'me' hangs on to. It clings to its self-importance. Without 'my' healthy outlook on life, family will suffer.

Look at the condition of the apparent world. Observe the myriad beliefs of every conceivable ilk and kind. Behind every belief there is a 'me' or an 'I' standing firm in support of 'his' or 'her' ideology.

People killing each other over beliefs!

That which is illusory must believe. It is compelled to believe. It will die to believe.

The 'I' says, "I would be so sad to no longer be here. I would miss my family and certainly, they would miss me. I firmly believe this."

It says, "My friends are important, how could I leave them?"

It clings, clutches and embraces its illusory nature. It conjures up heartbreaking stories that support its delusional importance, as if life itself depended on 'him' or 'her' for the sun to rise in the east.

There is no 'Jim', but 'my' apparent family enjoys a nice home. There is no 'Jim'; yet, friends seemingly enjoy the laughter or pain of what is being said or not said with this communication.

Things are generally quite relaxed.

Today a neighbor's dog destroyed a large branch on a very old bonsai maple tree 'I' carefully maintain. It was not a happy moment. 'I' assured the dog's owner it was simply an act of nature.

"It's what's happening," 'I' said.

Feelings of sadness arose. Fixing the little tree was attempted. Expressing 'my' apparent sadness with a friend ensued.

It appears that without the 'I' or 'me', seeming events are wild and unbridled; they apparently occur without care or compassion for apparent feelings.

Life happens full on!

Apparent family and friends--one and the same; unconditional love arising in all its seeming forms.

Nothing changes.

Everything changes.

Tonight 'I' asked *an old friend*, "Do you see anything different about the apparent 'me' these days?"

"You seem more social," she replied.

"Anything else," 'I' enquired.

"No, you seem pretty much the same," she said.

'I' would love to tell you how everything has changed, but no words arise that come close to describing this apparent metamorphosis.

Nothing has changed.

Can you see how impossible it is to describe the indescribable?

There is nothing new, yet everything is new.

Family and friends seem to sincerely enjoy asking questions and getting no answers.

'We' have fun together.

'We' laugh and cry

'We' fall and get up.

Aliveness, the wondrous joy of being alive, recognized (by no one) as 'This' which is always already, is 'That' which is and is not.

…becomes laughter for all.

Family and friends are reminded that what they have always been looking for is 'This' which is simply *what's happening.* There is nothing to get, for all is complete just as it is (and is not).

Daily News

Misery seems to drive the news.

Horror, sorrow and grief appear to be the norm transmitted from most networks on a daily basis.

Fear of nuclear war, mass shootings, disease, global warming, earthquakes, volcanoes, hurricanes, tornados and terrorism.

Fear of being sued, saying the wrong thing, being accused falsely, hammer us daily.

It seems like the 'me' thrives on trepidation.

'This' is what is happening.

Turn off the devise transmitting these images, sounds and commentaries.

Turn on.

Turn off.

Turn on.

Turn off.

Does anything change?

Different faces and locations, but similar events in what appears to be a real world.

...but the apparent world is not real or unreal.

There is just what seems to be happening.

Characters who believe they are real drive a world believed as real.

The apparent world is no more real than dreams during sleep.

The daily news, in the seeming waking state, would take issue with this assumption.

It would debate, introduce evidence, create high dramatic visual and auditory proof to protect its apparent incontrovertible existence.

How come you seem to know something we don't?

'I' do not know something 'you' don't.

There is simply no 'I' to know or not know; and no 'we' or 'you' to concur or not concur.

What is being suggested is really quite simple:

'I', 'me', 'you' is illusory.

...and that's that!

Anything and everything created by something illusory cannot be real or unreal.

...again, there is just what is happening.

...for no one.

All the perceived characters and events on the daily news are not separated by name or place.

It could be said there is only the absolute arising as whomever, whatever, wherever or however.

In other words:

• Wholeness appears as any and all characters.

• Unconditional love appears as pain or pleasure.

• Certainty appears as doubt or fear.

There is just this simple, inexplicable aliveness appearing as all those *things* we seem to see on the daily news.

Close is Far Away

The seeker might think 'he' or 'she' is getting close to 'This' freedom of unknowing, close to the utter relief of wholeness.

...but, how could that happen? There is only wholeness, unbounded unconditional love that is neither here nor there.

How can an apparent person be close to 'This' which is everything and nothing simultaneously?

How can anyone be close to that which already is 'This'?

It is simply impossible to be close, or even closer than close. Being close would require a separate self to know or experience being close.

Likewise, it is inconceivable that an apparent person could be *far away* from

'This' which is always already whole and free.

Searching ceases.

Seeking terminates.

Investigating and exploring our *true nature* becomes as irrelevant as the need to take care of an eleventh toe.

Meditating on the *Holi Name* becomes ludicrous; however it can be good for your posture.

Maintaining intense presence in the *Now* ripens, flowers and dissipates with the cessation of time.

Praying to *whomever or whatever* holds its own as a basic, stress releasing exercise; thus, it can make you feel better.

Finding the answer in $E=mc^2$ can be gloriously distracting and/or good brain exercise.

Basically all of the aforementioned require an 'I', a 'me' that believes 'it' has a long way to go and, conversely, that it is getting very close.

Close to what?

Far from what?

How can there be close to 'This' which is happening and not happening already?

How can there be far from 'This', which is always already, sans space or time?

The glorious wonder of wholeness, wild and free appearing as anything and everything, relaxes—apparently.

Lucent Store Rewards

'I' go out of my way to have a kind lady scan my groceries.

"Do you have your rewards card?"

"Yes," 'I' say smiling.

"Thank you," she responds.

Radiance shines and seems to light up the store…

…wholeness appearing as subtly as the wind through trees.

…unconditional love appears as vibrant aliveness.

It is so much fun to see her smile and hear her say, "Hi"!

…and she says it with enthusiasm!

Enthusiasm!

How can it get any better than that?

A gush of sunshine on a rainy day.

'I' am just one customer.

The unconditional love she is sharing with thousands of shoppers glistens from behind her new glasses.

She asked what goji berries tasted like and 'I' said, "Juicy-tangy," but could not describe the indescribable flavor of the Himalayas that is characteristic of this delectable berry.

So, next Thursday 'I' will take her some.

The apparent 'Jim' will take the seeming 'check-out lady' some berries.

Isn't it wonderful?

Nothing has to be done. Just go through the line, offer some divine fruit and smile.

Unconditional love rings and sings, and I get store rewards, *plus* some miles on my Alaska credit card as a bonus.

Nothing needs to be done.

Nothing will be done.

No 'Jim' to have any expectations.

No 'cashier' to accept or reject the seeming 'Jim'.

Just potent vibrant aliveness appearing to happen.

'I' will see my *checkout line grocer* Thursday at Fred Meyer!

Yippee!

'I' will have an eternity of maybe a minute…

But wait.

See it's like this…

There is no time.

Wholeness, the absolute, unconditional love simply arises for no one.

'This' is what is happening.

…and since there is no 'me', there is no 'her'.

Isn't it grand to be living the freedom of unknowing?

All the great stuff of an apparent rich, full life arises for no one.

The beauty of an apparent woman, as lovely as the wildflowers adorning Mt.

Rainier on a summer day, nourishes the seeming world.

Scintillating and indescribable is 'This' Freedom.

Smoke and Haze

Blue smoke envelopes the trees, hides the mountains, chokes the lungs.

Hazardous air warnings for all people is commonplace.

Over and over one hears:

"It never used to be this way!"

"Terrible, isn't it!"

"Global warming."

"Trumps fault."

"Armageddon."

"I can't breathe."

"Help!"

My favorite camp spot and the place on the planet I most enjoyed, Terwilliger Hot Springs, besieged by wildfires.

'This' is what is happening.

The natural reality heating and burning.

Animals simply lying low, exerting less energy.

Smoke and haze, neither good nor bad, apparently arising.

The apparent human lying low, exerting less energy.

No wishing it wasn't so.

Simply loving what's happening with a little help from an N95 particle respirator and a MinusA2 Air Purifier!

'I' Lose Again

It does not matter who, what, when why or how. The body seems to feel, the brain appears to think.

Any situation will do.

Jim plays chess.

However, there is no longer a 'Jim' who plays chess.

Playing chess happens.

It seems.

The brain thinks.

The body reacts.

Simple moves to begin.

Utter complexity very soon.

The game is either won or lost; yet there is no one who can win or lose.

Jim works on the house.

He throws away what seems to be excessive materialism but revered as treasure by another.

Others react with passive aggression.

Threats.

The body reacts.

The brain thinks.

Memories of cowardice arise.

Fear thoughts appear.

For who?

No 'me', yet uncomfortable thoughts and feelings arise.

For no one!

In the apparent world of 'me' winning seems to be all there is.

Losing seems to be attached to a brain set that is phenomenally unattractive.

The brain thinks and the body feels in any and all seeming situations.

Winning or losing still translates as unconditional love.

The human seems to want to shed pain as fast as possible; yet, pain is nothing but unconditional love arising as apparent discomfort on a scale of one through ten.

Physical or emotional, it does not matter, unconditional love is what is and is not.

'I' lose again.

'I' play again.

Apparently.

Never has there been an 'I' to play or lose.

Never.

Playing happens.

On the world stage one observes chaos, pain and destruction unimaginable to a small child or large adult.

The *so-called* adult tries to cope with losing everything, or he/she battles the psychological fear of losing it all.

It is difficult, perhaps impossible to deal and cope with climate change and its alarming connection with pristine forests burning down, major cities flooding or polar bears invading small communities for lack of ice.

Inconceivable for full grown adults to imagine the level of cruelty inflicted on humans **by** humans who believe they have an actual connection with God.

...still, the human keeps playing.

Winning sometimes...

Losing sometimes...

The glorious beauty of 'This' freedom of unknowing does not make either better or worse.

It is simply recognized by no one that winning and losing are constructs of the brain and have no actual existence.

So, take the pain of a wrong move.

Move again.

It does not matter.

This love is all there is.

There is no 'I' who has to "Suck it up" and somehow go on.

Wondrous aliveness cannot be conjugated or reduced down into its lowest terms.

It is *simply this...*

Ringing in the ears.

Guitar sounds in the other room.

The breath through the nose.

Fingers on a keyboard.

Dogs barking.

'This' freedom is not what seems to be happening physically or mentally.

'*Simply this*' which can and cannot be put into words.

How could it be better (or worse) that this?

A slight smile.

The eyes blink.

'You' win again?

No 'you' to win.

No 'I' to lose.

How refreshing.

No inner game.

No outer game.

No actual game at all!

Just the pleasure of a large brain creating.

Rest Day

It's just so amazing. The freedom of 'This', which is everything already, puts an ease to the low, lethargic energy apparently arising in the body and mind.

The body wants low activity and the brain is leaning towards rest.

There is just the simplicity of breathing and the mystery of thought arising.

Words such as *awareness, presence* or *now* do not work in the attempt to describe 'This' magnificence.

Consciousness does not do it.

No words can do it.

The head tilts slightly to the right, the eyes close and 'This' is it.

The hand goes to the cheek, the breath rises and falls, and the obvious wonder of aliveness rings.

Contentment.

For no one.

Peace.

As is.

Well-being.

Is 'This'.

Free.

Alive.

Bang.

Big bang!

Massage the scalp, rub the face, chuckle lightly.

'This' is and is not.

Indescribable.

Time for bed.

Certainty

Certainty is 'This', which appears to resonate as ineffable, wild and free aliveness; yet, no one is certain!

Wholeness, the absolute, unconditional love, certainty, apparently arising as anything and everything for no reason whatsoever.

Absolutely unknowable.

It is obvious!

So obvious...

...but, guess what?

There is no one here who knows that!

Yet, certainty arises.

...with no meaning

...and no purpose.

Then how can you be certain?

'I' cannot be certain; yet, certainty is what is apparently happening and, of course, what is apparently not happening.

Perhaps it can be said there is an uncertain certainty for no one.

Incredible, incorruptible freedom sings.

The freedom of unknowing appears to outshine the sun; darkness seemingly shimmers.

Never could 'I' have dreamed or imagined what is being implied with these words.

Certainty.

Absolute certainty.

...but 'I' cannot tell you of that in which there is certainty, for there is no 'I' to be certain or to harbor doubt.

It is not a feeling nor is it an experience.

There is not something 'I' can point to or allude to as a point of reference; who would point and to what?

Sitting is happening, fingers typing words...nothing going on...

Certainty could translate as the absolute or wholeness; words always fall short of that in which and to which they point.

It is not strength, but--oh--the strength!

If there was a way to *reach through* and show you it would be done, but there is no you to see.

...and there is no one here to reach through that which does not exist.

Some people say to me, "It must be so frustrating for you to not be able to tell us or show us what is so obvious to you."

...but frustration does not arise, for who would be frustrated?

...nor is there any semblance of loneliness in not having any immediate peers to share the comradery of this certainty.

The aliveness, seemingly inherent in this certainty, is nuclear.

...but, no one is certain; there is only certainty.

No answers as to what life is all about...

No direction given...

No meaning derived...

Just the obvious certainty of 'This', which cannot be described, warming the apparent body and mind with unconditional love.

It's not as if 'I' know or have discovered something; to know or discover would require something or somebody to do so which suggests separation.

'This', that is always already, is just so utterly evident.

'That' or 'This' in which all sincere seekers yearn and long for is 'This' already.

Outright certainty!

Bountiful wholeness!

Outrageous freedom!

Absolute certainty of 'This' (that is and is not) which cannot be explained, talked about, identified or illustrated...

For no one...

Freedom so profound it grows untouched by apparent man or beast.

Impossible to know...

...for there is no one to know.

The body/mind configuration falls to its apparent knees and simply laughs at the sheer simplicity of this glorious aliveness.

"Oh, the joy of unknowing!"

Bothersome Delays

A typical *modern world person* might be:

Sitting at a gas station waiting for an attendant who is engaged in three conversations.

Keyboarding an important document and a simple computer issue shuts him or her down.

Driving comfortably for hours and suddenly stopped by two mile per hour traffic.

Sitting in the middle of high emotional drama with no escape route.

Waiting in long lines for food, banking, post office, doctor appointment, Department of Motor Vehicles, ski lift...

The list, of course, goes on and on...

The apparent point is this:

Ordinary activities have a seeming beginning, middle and end. People want to get to the end and get on with the <u>next</u> thing.

However, there is no *next thing*.

'This' freedom has no time.

It is impossible to have a beginning, middle and end.

There is no one to begin.

So called <u>ordinary things</u> are what is happening (and not happening).

How can what already is (and is not) be better or worse? It is already what it is.

There is no space in 'This' freedom.

How could what already is (and is not) be here or there?

Up or down?

In or out?

Front or back?

Have value or lack of value?

It is 'This' already.

Wholeness.

Energy.

Non-duality.

Freedom.

Nothing appearing or disappearing.

Simply this extraordinarily ordinary, unconditional aliveness blazing.

No ego riding along.

No brain having to create a 'me'.

Just living, unconditional love thriving.

Nothing *bothers* that which is not.

Feelings, thoughts and emotions arise.

All three are 'This' which is and is not already.

'This' is what is happening and what is not happening.

'I' think 'I' will brush my teeth now.

(No 'I' *to* think; no now for events to occur.)

'This' is.

'This' wholeness cannot even be called an adventure, even though the brain and body seem to be flying faster than the speed of light!

Stupendous freedom!

Thank you!

Thanking simply happens for no one.

No one thanking and nothing being thanked.

Just "Thank you".

Pain and Pleasure

When the apparent 'Jim' seemingly disappeared, it wasn't long before pain and pleasure seemed to be happening concurrently!

'I' have attempted to describe this to various friends but have met with no apparent success in doing so.

Pain happens.

Sensations occur.

No matter what words we affix to this phenomenon it, of course, cannot describe what the apparent body or mind appears to be experiencing.

Falling and hitting the head hurts. Usually when this happens other body parts such as fingers, elbows, knees or ankles get involved.

Thoughts arise.

Words blurt from our mouths that can be exceptionally ill-favored.

The *love of our life* leaves.

She's gone; 'one' is left with the scent of her last stick of incense burning on the kitchen table.

Falling onto the knees, her name blurts from the mouth, "L.....!"

The apparent pain unbearable.

Images of her eyes arise of how she looked at you when she would say, "I love You."

Tears.

Tears.

Tears.

Oh, the excruciating heartache!

Crying happens.

There is fullness in this apparent agony that can only translate as unconditional love.

Something and nothing in seeming tandem.

Can 'we' be miserable and euphoric simultaneously?

Only if 'we' see ourselves trapped in time.

That is impossible.

There is no 'me' and obviously no time.

Simultaneous does not work in this description.

Unconditional love is not a something in time or space. It is not an *it*.

Pleasure and pain are, of course, words.

There is only wholeness.

It is obvious and simple to see how pleasure and pain have no separation.

The emptiness of a *lost love* is the fullness of unconditional love.

It is recognized by no one to be non-dual, that is, seemingly, our worst pain is our greatest pleasure apparently happening in pristine synchronicity.

I say apparently because there are not two to be *in synch*.

Pain and pleasure are one and the same.

Wholeness appearing as pain; yet, joy is that pain.

Indescribable.

Nobody Loves No one

Isn't that the truth! Although there is no truth to be known, "Nobody loves no one" is a statement readily apropos for what is being suggested in this writing.

No 'I' to meet someone like 'you'.

Most people say, "*I want to meet someone like you.*"

No 'me' to fall in love with 'you'.

Most people say, "*I want to fall in love with someone like you*".

No 'you' for 'me' to fall in love.

Most people say, "*I'm in love with 'you'*".

No 'I'.....no 'you'...

...to fall in love

    ...to fall in love

        ...to fall in love

Love

Love

Love

Is all there is

...and

is not.

There is nobody to love someone.

Just unconditional love translating into the freedom of unparalleled aliveness.

'This' breathtaking aliveness apparently taking shape as anything, everything and nothing for no one,

Most people say, *"I am someone and someone loves 'me'."*

Nobody to be somebody!

...but it feels that way.

Oh, 'I' know how that feels.

The freedom of unknowing is all you have longed and waited for.

'I' know...but 'I' can't...let go.

There is no 'you' to know or let go.

I want that freedom.

There is no freedom just as there is no 'I'.

Freedom is another word for the indescribable party, the endless bogie, of 'That' or 'This' which is already.

'This' freedom is all there is (and is not).

Nobody loves no one; yet, unconditional love thrives as 'This' aliveness.

Nothing to attain.

Indubitable love, which is, cannot be sought.

Impossible to seek 'This' which is not a narrow moment called *now*.

Any attempt to grasp 'That' which has no space is futile.

Oh...

The peace.

What's Going On?

I mean, sigh, there's 'me', but no 'me', and no one gets that. 'I' don't get that! What other words can be used?

'This' is nothing, but everything arises. The silent gazing, groping for the right words to describe all that is and is not.

Even when the apparent 'me' is discovered, but not discovered to be illusory, the right words do not appear.

A magic potion does not suddenly appear, nor does any form of newly discovered clarity.

It seems that to have any semblance of what is happening, there must be what is not happening.

This, however, could become tedious for the reader; but it is obvious that no one, including the apparent author, has any idea what is being suggested in this communication.

Research cannot uncover what is being said in this message. How could one find anything on the subject? 'This', which is nothing and everything, is always already.

There is no longer even the slightest inkling of desire for anything, anywhere, anyhow!

Aliveness happens. It is 'This', which has no explanation and cannot be spoken of in terms of being something objective.

If there were to be an 'I' or 'me', which there is not, it would be 'This' which is timeless and space less.

There is no 'me' to say, 'I' am 'me'; yet, an apparent person, with the name 'Jim' is typing these words.

So, of course 'I' am here, but 'I' am not. There is no 'I' to be am.

Even to ask the question "Who am I" is ludicrous and irrelevant.

It's like asking the fog to solidify into a substance that somehow stays put and behaves like something apparently stable and concrete.

Nonetheless, there is an apparent person with the name 'Jim' attached, that seemingly functions in an apparent world.

However, there is no person who apparently stands separate and knows that.

Wholeness, oneness, being free, simply appears as an individual.

Unimaginable!

Who would be there to imagine the unimaginable?

It's all so wonderfully unknowable.

The leaves of early May bring an apparent fresh fullness to the forest.

...but, so what?

Alone.

Feeling down.

The *blues.*

Nobody cares.

Ah, gee...

'I' don't care.

Boo, hoo...

Sun is shining, sky is blue, slight breeze through trees.

Solitude appearing dramatically.

Don't know what to do, where to go or who to call.

There's no 'me' to get therapy, pray to god, meditate within.

'This' is the end of the line baby!

Can't even cry but wish 'I' could.

Not drawn to alcohol, drugs or changes.

Downhearted, miserably low, painfully crestfallen; mental and physical sensations seeming to appear for no one.

Bummed out!

Not looking for a way out or through.

Various four-letter expletives arise in the brain and some spill from the mouth.

Tightness in the stomach.

Flat faced.

Humorless.

Crack the neck; breathe.

Fizzy brooding, bubbling and bursting.

No fear, no desire.

No past, no future.

No here, no now.

Just because there is no longer an 'I', a 'me', doesn't mean the body/mind ceases to seemingly undergo misery on occasion.

That's for sure!

Oh, man.

Let's get something to eat.

Heart aches.

Then the daily news…

Does not help.

Nothing helps.

How could anything help?

There is no one to help!

'This' is what's happening.

Doleful thoughts…

Tender feelings…

Arising…

…but, so what?

Serious

It's this seriousness that works into the apparent pores. The 'me' thinks it is real and takes on a solemn reference for itself.

'I am' serious, take me seriously. 'I' know what 'I' am talking about.

Everywhere one looks, apparent people are taking themselves seriously.

The prison of seriousness confines and strangles even children into various shades of anger and resentment; yet, mysteriously, spectrums of unconditional love dissolve the apparent person.

There may be seriousness, but with no 'I' or 'me' to *own* it, seriousness seemingly arises for a while.

There is no one to ask the question, "Who or what is it that is aware and serious about it?"

Seriousness arises and may seem like a wrinkly forehead, half open eyes, flat, solemn face, accented with the aches and pains accrued with the living mileage of life.

Is a waterfall, sunset, or ocean breeze serious? Any of the three would have to stand apart, be aware and pass some sort of judgment to make it so.

People ask 'me' if 'I' believe in what is being said, and they are serious in every respect. They want to know, in the worst way, what 'This' is; they want to know if 'I' am serious with any of the suggestions being made in this communication.

'I' may appear serious, but how could this message ever be communicated? There is an apparent 'Jim' who may appear serious, but since there is no actual 'Jim', there is simply serious laughter, apparently.

The wonder of that which is 'This' already, speaks in the serious tone of unconditional love.

Maybe 'I' should go into *stand-up comedy*. Everything that is apparently said and not said just sounds ridiculous, comedic and strange.

Some say that what is being expressed in this dialog entails the complete absence of logic and reason.

Some say it simply sounds like one has lost touch with reality.

Some say there is not a single word of truth spoken one could take as serious and credible.

Seriously folks, you aren't real (but you seriously think you are).

No 'me', no 'you' no truth.

Just this outrageous freedom pulsating with an indescribable aliveness for no one.

Seriously!

So Much Spiritualism

Advaita Vedanta, Pure Conscious Awareness, The Now, Self Enquiry, Nisargadatta Maharaj, Ramana Maharshi, Kashmir Shaivism, Enlightenment, Sages, Perfect Masters of Non-Dualism...

Ahhh, stop it, just stop it!

What is being suggested in this discourse has nothing, absolutely nothing to do with anything spiritual.

It is about as far away from spiritualty as it is close.

It is not Holi.

It is not special.

It is not even non-dual. What would non-dual even be but another concept, another idea?

It is not even an *It*.

This message simply points to the obvious aliveness of what is and is not.

It is ludicrous to see people claiming to be non-dual masters.

Masters of what?

The absurdity of those claiming to be enlightened is astounding!

What could become enlightened?

WHAT?

Inconceivable!

There is just 'This' aliveness.

There is no one.

No 'me'.

No 'you'.

No 'others'.

Those apparent realized beings...

Hmmm...

Might they be upholding and supporting an illusion for their own gain?

Even if that is true, it is simply what is happening.

Wholeness appearing as enlightened, realized beings making a profit.

There is no right or wrong, good or bad.

'This' Freedom is all there is and is not, but there is no one who is free.

There is just unconditional, lovely freedom.

It is so free and does not even know it.

What could know it?

Who could know it?

No heaven.

No Hell.

No Holi Name.

No afterlife.

Thank you.

There is no 'you' being thanked, but the expression of *Thank You* feels marvelous.

Marvelous!

No one can get 'This'.

There is no one **to** get 'This'.

Freedom rings.

It rings so loudly; yet, it is quiet.

For no one.

All Thoughts Welcome

Thoughts arise.

What else needs to be said?

Without the 'me' or 'I' thoughts are benign and powerless.

A thought comes.

A thought goes.

Good and bad thoughts do not exist.

There are just apparent thoughts.

None of them real or unreal.

Many people believe that to have unwanted fearful thinking is a sign of weakness.

It is obvious, when the 'me' is no more, all beliefs vanish like early morning fog. There is simply no 'self' to have a belief.

Look at the condition of the apparent world.

Beliefs are running the show!

Illusion is calling the shots literally and figuratively.

Unimaginable sorrow and violence, based on someone's imagination of how things are supposed to be, prevails.

It is just so simple.

The 'me' is the problem.

Why is 'me' the problem?

It believes it is real, lives in a real world, and has the free will and choice to do something about it.

All of it arising as thought that adheres to the illusory 'me' which has no credible existence.

Thought plays the major role in enabling the delusive nature of an imagined self to run wild.

My god!

The thought arises, "You're getting to serious."

...and then it is gone.

Some thing does not become too serious.

It seems that the illusory 'me' is made of tar, hot tar. Anything and everything can and will, apparently, stick to its perceived body and mind.

This tar, body-mind, configuration accumulates an apparent viscous shell so thick any semblance of the delight of simple aliveness is impossible.

How does one free him or her self from this apparent trap?

One does not free him or her self. There is no self to become free.

There is just freedom and the wonder of aliveness already.

You cannot get 'This'.

Everything and nothing is already 'This'.

The individual cannot look for 'This' which is already 'This'.

Straight down.

Straight down.

Straight down.

Falling faster than fast.

No chance to grasp or grab anything.

No chance to look around and take in the view.

No possibility to even gasp.

Over and out!

End of the Line

Since there are no beginnings, endings are impossible.

Aliveness happens, apparently.

The magnificence of seeming solitude reveals itself as nothing and everything dancing and singing around, on or in an invisible campfire of unconditional love.

The end of 'me' is the end of *the end*.

Questions cease.

Thoughts may arise that appear as questions but go unanswered.

The *end of the line* shows no mercy or compassion.

It is so difficult; yet, so easy and simple.

Because there is no actual end, life takes on an intensity that is unimaginable.

In the story of 'me' there is always the seeking and planning to alleviate feelings of loneliness.

Without the 'me' loneliness is no more, but the intensity of seeming aloneness arises.

Thoughts emerge of animals in pairs or flowers and bees ; yet, the wonder of nothing and everything, in apparent duality, is recognized as wholeness appearing as two.

What the apparent person does or does not do with this freedom is, in actuality, irrelevant.

No person, no freedom.

There is simply 'This' aliveness, seemingly in what is called a human body, writing.

It sounds like this message should be shared, but no one calls or knocks on my door.

Understandable.

This communication cannot be communicated.

...and, since nothing happens, nothing can be shared.

'This', to some, would appear to be nirvana, heaven, liberation, enlightenment; but it is not.

Heaven, liberation, and so on, pale as words in trying to describe the essence of 'This', which is already.

Believe me, 'This' is not at the end of the line!

Fear gone.

Never was.

Anxiety.

A seven-letter word.

Stress.

Non-existent.

Worry.

What is that?

Doubt.

Reserved for a 'me', 'I' or 'you'.

Problems.

None.

Solutions.

Zero, for there are no problems.

Breathe, breathe in the air.

Take the pulse.

Stretch the back.

Do whatever you like.

There is no *will be*, just as there is no *has* been. It is, therefore, impossible to gather in enough *tomorrows* only to find you have stockpiled nothing but a lot of desolate *yesterdays.*

There is not even now.

No metaphorical train traveling to the end of the line.

Just 'This' whooping aliveness apparently happening for no one!

Get in it.

Celebrate being alone.

For you see, there is no being alone.

Alone connotes separation.

There is only wholeness.

No parts or pieces.

Simply the absolute.

Appearing as the end.

Seemingly saying,

"Thank you."

"Talk to you again soon!"

Glossary

Apostrophes

I, me or self, as we commonly refer to ourselves and believe as real, is represented as 'I', 'me', 'self', 'you', 'Jim' etc. Apostrophes are used to connote the apparent falseness of this assumption and, most importantly, to suggest that this 'self' is illusory; it is not what it appears to be.

To illustrate: 'I' or 'me' is illusory; it is a psychosomatic misunderstanding.

Potent aliveness, wholeness, the absolute, unconditional love, certainty or that which cannot be described, is represented by the pronoun 'This'. Apostrophes are used to connote the aforementioned and to suggest the depth and beauty of 'This' which is already.

To illustrate: 'This' unconditional love can appear as potent, vibrant aliveness.

'This' absolute, empty-fullness is wild, free and appears as a fire in the sky sunset.

Apparent

Apparent and seeming suggest there is no real person or world; wholeness is all there is and is not. Apparent could be used in every sentence throughout the book and in most cases it is used as a reminder to the reader that everything is apparent.

To illustrate: The apparent world suffers.

The seeming 'self' believes it is real.

An apparent book is being written by the seeming 'Jim'.

Italics

In some chapters there may be a second person either asking a question, making a comment or taking part in an apparent conversation; these enrichments will be italicized.

To illustrate:

Why bother reading or discussing this?

Exactly!

Ludicrous!

...but, you are writing a book.

No, sorry, but a book is being written...apparently.

So many ideas and opinions!

Seems so, doesn't it?

Yes, it certainly does.

About the Author

Jim Galbraith currently resides in Milwaukie, Oregon, a small community on the outskirts of Portland.

'He' shares his home with son Josh, Carrie, Josh's wife, grandsons Maxwell and Zakkary, dogs Bruno, Maxdog and Zoey, cats Loki and Leah, U-turn the turtle, two fighting fish with a goldfish guard and some well cared for Bonsai trees.

A few things 'Jim' likes:

The potent vibrant aliveness of

…rain

…rushing wind through trees

…the feel of a smile

…the freedom of laughter

…black recliner and ottoman

…aches and pains

…a deep, full, satisfying breath

…anything and everything that seems to arise for no one.

'Jim' is as happy washing dishes or paying taxes as he is skiing down the perfect slope with excellent snow or feeling warm and cozy in his bed on a cold morning.

'He' is an apparent man and is usually relieved of seeming worldly stress and fear; however, he might curse in slow, heavy traffic but smile at the same time (or shortly thereafter).

'Jim' loves talking about 'This' freedom of unknowing that, of course, cannot be talked about, which, in turn, sparks laughter quite often!

Currently 'Jim' does not speak or give talks. 'He' is a common man living a simple, ordinary life in the peace of anonymity.

Printed in Great Britain
by Amazon